SNAPPY PUT-DOWNS & FUNNY INSULTS

BY
JOSEPH ROSENBLOOM

ILLUSTRATIONS BY JOYCE BEHR

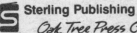

Sterling Publishing Co., Inc.   New York
Oak Tree Press Co., Ltd.   London & Sydney

Also by Joseph Rosenbloom
Illustrated by Joyce Behr

Bananas Don't Grow on Trees
Biggest Riddle Book in the World
Daffy Dictionary
Doctor Knock-Knock's Official Knock-Knock
  Dictionary
Gigantic Joke Book
How Do You Make an Elephant Laugh?
Monster Madness
Polar Bears Like It Hot
Silly Verse (and even Worse)

Library of Congress Cataloging in Publication Data
Rosenbloom, Joseph.
  Snappy put-downs & funny insults.

  Includes index.
  Summary: A collection of insulting remarks (none
malicious) to use as put-downs for any occasion,
e.g.: Why don't you put an egg in your shoe and beat it.
  1. Invective—Anecdotes, facetiae, satire, etc.
2. Wit and humor, Juvenile. [1. Invective—Anecdotes,
facetiae, satire, etc. 2. Jokes] I. Behr, Joyce.
II. Title.
PN6231.I65R57   818'.5402   80-54348
ISBN 0-8069-4646-6   AACR2
ISBN 0-8069-4647-4 (lib. bdg.)

Special School Book Fair Edition

Copyright © 1981 Joseph Rosenbloom
Published by Sterling Publishing Co., Inc.
Two Park Avenue, New York, N.Y. 10016
Distributed in Australia by Oak Tree Press Co., Ltd.
660 George Street, Sydney 2000, N.S.W.
Distributed in the United Kingdom
by Ward Lock Ltd., 47 Marylebone Lane, London W1M 6AX
Manufactured in the United States of America
Library of Congress Catalog Card No.: 80-54348

CONTENTS

To
David and Sandy Backerman
with love

1 GO to your CAGE!

People know of you by word of mouth—yours.

You're a sight for sore eyes—a real eyesore!

I wish you would get lost some place where they have no "found" department.

You must use gunpowder on your face. It looks shot.

Your mouth is like a mailbox—open day and night.

You've heard of permanent press. Well, what you're wearing looks like permanent mess.

I can read you like a book. How I wish I could shut you up like one!

You look like a million—every day of it.

One more wrinkle and you could pass for a prune.

So! That's what a mummy looks like without bandages!

You have what it takes. The only trouble is you've had it too long.

Is that your face, or are you wearing a ski mask?

You could talk your head off and never miss it.

If you had to eat your words, you'd get ptomaine poisoning.

A stocking over your face would look better than over your legs.

I've seen nicer hair on mops.

You couldn't be two-faced or you wouldn't be wearing the one you have on now.

I hear you were going to have your face lifted, but when you found out the price—you let the whole thing drop.

Your mind needs changing. It's filthy.

The last time I saw someone like you, I had to pay admission.

With friends like you, who needs enemies?

You look wonderful. Who is your embalmer?

The only time you had a figure was when you had the mumps.

The closest you'll ever get to becoming the toast of the town is a sunburn.

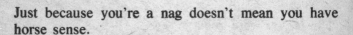

If you stopped using dirty words, you'd have nothing to say.

Just because you're a nag doesn't mean you have horse sense.

I've never seen your tongue. It moves too fast.

I hear you're not allowed to visit the zoo. Your face scares the animals.

You look like a million dollars—all green and wrinkled.

Your outfit fits you like a glove—a catcher's mitt.

Time may heal a lot of things, but it hasn't done you much good.

You're so neat—not a wrinkle out of place.

Your face is so wrinkled, you should have it pressed.

You remind me of history—always repeating yourself.

You're a real bargain—50% off.

The day you were born you cried like a baby. So did your parents.

No wonder you have headaches. Your halo is on too tight.

If anyone said hello to you—you'd be stuck for an answer.

Anybody who said he was crazy about you—would have to be.

Tell me, do you sleep with your face in the pillow to be kind to burglars?

You'd leave your head in bed in the morning if it weren't attached to your neck.

Why don't you hop on your broom and fly away?

2 SHALL WE FENCE?

My doctor told me to exercise with dumbbells. Shall we fence?

I wouldn't say you're a perfect idiot. No one is perfect.

I know I am talking like an idiot. I have to talk that way so you can understand me.

The sharpest thing about you is your tongue.

Keep your mouth shut. My plants are wilting.

You may not be light on your feet, but you certainly are light in your head.

Until I met you, I thought blood was thicker than water.

You remind me of a one-story building—nothing upstairs.

If you were a building, you'd be condemned.

You couldn't be as stupid as you look—and live.

You shouldn't have trouble falling asleep. You're unconscious most of the time anyway.

The trouble with you is that you're forgotten —but not gone.

Why don't you put an egg in your shoe and beat it?

You don't have an inferiority complex. You're just inferior.

Some people have savoir faire. You don't even have carfare.

You must have a sixth sense. There's no sign of the other five.

A thought struck you once: you were in the hospital for a month.

You remind me of a jigsaw puzzle—so many of the pieces are missing.

You seem to have plenty of get-up-and-go. So, why don't you?

Could I drop you off somewhere—say, the roof?

You're good-looking in a way
—away off.

It was nice visiting your neighborhood. I enjoy slumming.

Just because you go around in circles doesn't make
you a big wheel.

I know why you never go on a vacation. You're
always on an ego trip.

You have only two faults: everything you do and
everything you say.

If you have your life to do over again—don't!

I never forget a face, and in your case, I'll remember both of them.

You must be crazy, not because you talk to yourself, but because you listen.

If I gave you an eraser, would you rub yourself
out?

Why don't you go out and play in the traffic?

You are the most complete
nothing since the invention
of the zero.

Would you mind closing the door—from the outside?

If you went to the zoo, people would try to feed
you.

You can go back home now. They finished cleaning
your cage.

Is that your face or are you breaking it in for a
bulldog?

I'd like to help you out. Which way did you come in?

3 HOCUS POCUS

Did I miss you when you were gone? I didn't know you were gone.

Give me time. I'll find a way of ignoring you.

Why don't you drink some spot remover and disappear!

I expect you to go places—and the sooner the better.

People like you don't grow on trees—they swing from them.

You must get up early. How else could you say so many stupid things in one day?

I can depend on you. You're always around when you need me.

For a minute I thought you were crazy. I was wrong. You've been crazy for much longer than that.

I came to see you off—and you certainly are.

You've given me something to live for—revenge.

One of us is crazy. But don't worry, I'll keep your secret.

You remind me of a goat—always butting in.

You should go to Hollywood. The walk will do you good.

You're a regular information bureau—always telling people where to go.

How can I miss you if you won't go away?

If you lived by your wits, you'd starve.

They say there's a fuel shortage, but you're the biggest fuel (fool) I've ever seen.

You have a mechanical mind. Too bad so many of the screws are missing.

You never change your mind. You flush it.

Keep this under your hat. I know you've got plenty of room there.

I hear you had to drop out of kindergarten—couldn't keep up with the work.

You have a baby face—and a mind to match.

Anyone who looks like you ought to be arrested for disturbing the peace.

 You're nasty, disagreeable, stupid, repulsive, obnoxious—and those are your good points.

Please don't talk when I'm interrupting.

You have such a swelled head, you must have your hats made in a tent factory.

Something is preying on your mind. But don't worry, it will soon die of starvation.

Why don't you rub vanishing cream all over yourself and disappear?

Why don't you cross the street blindfolded?

Why don't you make like a pack of cards and shuffle off?

4 DISORDER in the COURT

"Call out the narcotics squad— 165 pounds of dope just walked in!"

You are wearing shoes to match your personality: sneakers.

If I were in your shoes—I'd shine them.

You have a mind like a streak of lightning—fast and crooked.

You're so crooked, you have to screw your head on every morning.

The only time you're on the level is when you're asleep.

I've got to hand it to you, you're always trying— very trying.

You're not a juvenile delinquent—just an active, precocious young person with homicidal tendencies.

I hear they named a cake after you—crumb.

You have more crust than a whole pie factory.

Why be disagreeable? With a little more effort, you could be a real stinker.

You have an arresting personality, and you should be arrested for it.

You should work for the post office—even your brain is cancelled.

You're like a railroad train—plain loco and no motive.

Where did you get your brains—at the bird store?

You've been in hot water so much, you look like a teabag.

You've been in more hot water than a boiled egg.

You've been in so many jams, you could be spread on bread.

Make like scissors and cut out!

You're a real gyp
off the old block.

What you need is a
pat on the back—
often enough and
low enough.

You'd be a real
charmer if it
weren't for your
personality.

Don't think it
hasn't been
pleasant knowing you
—because it hasn't!

You have a fine mind, and anyone with a mind like
yours should be fined.

What does your mother do for a headache—send
you out to play?

You have more nerve than an infected tooth.

You never tell a lie when the truth will do more
damage.

The only regular exercise you get is stretching the truth.

You can't even tell the truth without lying.

Remember the fish: if he kept his mouth closed, he wouldn't get caught.

You had an unfortunate accident in childhood—you were born.

Your parents never struck you, except in self-defense.

Does the U.N. know about your face? It looks like an undeclared war.

You're nobody's fool, but maybe I can get someone to adopt you.

You started at the bottom—and stayed there.

I know twelve people who would like to meet you—a jury.

You're such a klutz, if you threw yourself on the floor, you'd miss.

I'd like to hear your opinion, but isn't there enough ignorance in the world already?

You remind me of someone important in history: the rear end of what Paul Revere rode on.

You don't want anyone to make a fuss over you—just to treat you as they would any celebrity.

I think you're the greatest, but then again, what do I know?

5 WHAT'S UP, DUCK?

 Have I met you someplace before? I sometimes get careless where I go.

If I had a face like yours, I'd walk backwards.

You have a face that looks like it wore out six bodies.

I never forget a face—but in your case, I'll make an exception.

Your head is getting too big for your toupee.

You're so conceited, you'd join the navy so the world could see you.

You remind me of the ocean. You never dry up.

I don't care what anyone says, I'll still talk to you.

I'd like to kick you in the teeth, but why improve your looks?

Stupid? I hear you even flunked recess.

Wipe your nose. Your brains are leaking!

Your brain has paused permanently for station identification.

You're as strong as an ox—and just about as intelligent.

You had to become the outdoor type. No one would let you inside.

You really have a head on your shoulders. Too bad it's on backwards.

I've seen better heads on cabbages.

I hear you went to see a lot of doctors to have your head examined, but they couldn't find anything.

The more I think of you, the less I think of you.

Don't worry about losing your mind. You'd never miss it.

Where have you been all my life—and when are you going back there?

You think you're a great traveller just because your mind is always wandering.

Travel broadens a person. You look like you've been all over the world.

I'd like to make a complaint about you, but I don't feel like standing in line.

Your name must be Bob—spelled with two *o*'s.

You made a big mistake today. You got out of bed.

You remind me of a retired postman—no zip.

I hear you were a sickly baby. Did you live?

I hear you were a beautiful baby. What happened?

Is that a recent condition—or were you born that way?

I've enjoyed talking to you. My mind needed the rest.

Why don't you make like a banana and split?

Things could be worse. You could be twins.

Don't give up. They'll find a cure for what's bothering you someday.

If I gave you a drum, would you beat it?

If I gave you a Kleenex, would you blow?

Why don't you let your hair grow—right over your face?

You have low voice and a mentality to match.

You're a perfect M.C.—(Mental Case).

Just because you dribble all over yourself doesn't make you a basketball player.

You deserve a big hand—right across the mouth.

You must have a large brain to hold so much ignorance.

Next time you give away your old clothes—stay in them.

Don't go away. I want to forget you exactly as you are.

6 SQUEAK UP!

Are you a man or a mouse? Squeak up!

I hear you were born on April 2nd—one day late.

How did you get here, wriggle off the hook?

I'd like to run into you again some time—when you're walking and I'm driving.

You think you're a comedian, but you ought to be gagged.

You're so funny, I can hardly keep from not laughing.

You're about as entertaining as one wrestler.

You're about as funny as an infected toenail.

Jokes like that will make humor illegal.

Even your jokes about old jokes are old.

You think you're funny, but you're only laughable.

I just contributed to a charity that might help you—the Mental Health Fund.

No wonder your mind is clear. It's not cluttered up with facts.

May I borrow your I.Q.? I'm going out with a moron tonight.

Your jokes are so corny, they could feed 200 chickens for five years.

You have a great future as a comedian. One look at you is enough to break anyone up.

You think you're a wit?
Well, you're half right.

I like what you're wearing,
but aren't you a little early
(late) for Halloween?

I'd tell you to stop acting
like a fool—but I don't
think you're acting.

You made that joke up all
by yourself out of your
head? You must be!

You remind me of a
chicken—always laying eggs.

If Adam came back to earth, the only things he
would recognize are your jokes.

You have a contagious laugh. People get sick when
they hear it.

Just keep on talking, so I'll know what you're not
thinking.

I hope you live to be as old as your jokes.

The last time I saw something like you, I pinned a tail on it.

I refuse to engage you in a battle of wits. I don't take advantage of the handicapped.

Why don't you sit down and take a mess off your feet?

Don't sit down too hard. You could give yourself a brain concussion.

You have a mechanical mind? Too bad it's never been wound up.

Don't go to a mind reader, go to a palmist. At least you know you've got a palm.

How would you like to be the first person to be kicked into orbit?

You're out of this world—and I hope you'll stay there.

Stop looking in the mirror. Haven't you ever seen a moron before?

You have a ready wit. Please let me know when it's ready.

The only thing bright about you is the seat of your pants.

I guess you're okay when people get to know you. But who wants to get to know you?

If your mouth were any bigger, you could talk into your ears.

If you bit your tongue, you'd die of acid poisoning.

Why don't you take a sight-seeing trip through a meat chopper?

Please play the guitar and stop picking on me.

Can I borrow your head for my rock garden?

What are you going to be—if the neighbors let you grow up?

Who do I think I'm talking to? How many guesses do I get?

What a snob! You go out in the garden so the flowers can smell you.

When you get back home, give my regards to the warden.

When I want your opinion, I'll rattle your cage.

I can take a joke pretty far. Where do you want to go?

7 HELLO, HOT LIPS!

You should have been born in the Dark Ages. You look awful in the light.

I could say nice things about you, but I'd rather tell the truth.

You have a striking personality. How long has it been on strike?

You'd make a good photographer—the way you snap at people.

Is that your face or is today Halloween?

You can improve the quality of this conversation by keeping your mouth shut.

I don't know what I'd do without you. It's fun thinking about it.

You're probably not as dumb as you look. You couldn't be.

Surprise me. Say something intelligent.

Who do I think I'm shoving? I don't know. What is your name?

Why don't you make like a tree and leave?

Why don't you go to an antique store? Maybe someone will buy you.

You have the face of a saint—a Saint Bernard.

There's only one thing wrong with your face: it's on the wrong end.

You have a face that looks better from the back.

You have that far-away look. The farther you get, the better you look.

You know, with the proper amount of coaching, you could be a nobody.

Please let me say goodbye until we never meet again.

If you have someplace to go—go!

I hope you never feel the way you look.

Your personality is so repulsive, even an echo wouldn't answer you.

You'd make a perfect stranger.

Help improve the neighborhood—move!

You don't know the meaning of the word fear. You're too scared to look it up.

Your visit has climaxed an already dull day.

You have a lovely color in your cheeks—green.

You're not yourself today. I noticed the improvement right away.

I admit that you're stronger than I am, but bad breath isn't everything.

Please don't change. Stay as stupid as you are.

You couldn't count to twenty without taking your shoes off.

Some people can tear a telephone book in half. You'd have trouble with a wet Kleenex.

You're so weak,
you couldn't bend
a wet noodle.

You're so weak,
you couldn't even
crack a joke.

You're in such bad shape, you couldn't jump to a conclusion.

You're in such bad shape, you couldn't clear your throat.

You're in such bad shape, you'd have trouble beating a rug.

The closest you'll ever get to being brave is to eat a hero sandwich.

You're such a coward, you're afraid to strike a bargain.

You're such a coward, you won't even strike a match.

Don't feel worthless. You can always be used as a horrible example.

Two is company. You're a crowd.

Want to see something funny? Look in the mirror.

Of course, you're not a coward.
You just have a low threshold
of pain.

You're not a coward. You just
can't stand the sight of blood—
yours.

I've heard so much about you. What's your side of
the story?

8 WHO AXED YOU?

Things could be worse. You could be here in person.

How long can a person live without a brain? How old are you?

You're ignorant, ugly, worthless, and stupid. But, then again, no one is perfect.

Please turn the other way. I have a sensitive stomach.

I loved your execution. In fact, I'm all in favor of it.

Let's talk again after your brain transplant.

You look much better with my eyes closed.

I believe in the hereafter—so hereafter, don't bother me.

The only thing strong about you is your breath.

Your idea of fun is a first-class funeral.

If you have such an open mind, why aren't you wearing a warm hat?

Let's see what kind of athlete you are. How about holding your breath for ten minutes?

Some people bring happiness wherever they go; you bring happiness whenever you go.

If anyone kicked you in the heart, they'd break their toe.

You may be a down-to-earth person, but you're not down far enough to suit me.

You have such a rotten personality—if you threw a boomerang, it wouldn't come back.

Tell me about yourself. I enjoy horror stories.

When you come into a room, the mice jump on a chair.

Broaden your mind. Put a stick of dynamite in each ear.

It takes all kinds of people to make up the world. Too bad you're not one of them.

If you tried to join the human race, you'd be turned down.

I'd like to know you better—if I can keep my stomach from turning.

You must be a tolerant person. How else could you stand yourself?

Say, is your heart in any way related to the snowman?

You have a nice personality—but not for a human being.

I won't ask you to behave like a human being. I know you don't do imitations.

As an outsider, what do you think of the human race?

Didn't I see your face before on a bottle of iodine?

Why don't you crawl back under your rock?

You look fine to me. Now, let me put the lights on.

Have you looked at yourself in the mirror lately—or are you a coward?

You have one of those mighty minds—mighty empty.

You're such a sourpuss, when you suck a lemon—the lemon makes faces.

9 MURDER on the HIGH C's!

When you sing it reminds me of pirates—murder on the high C's.

We have a cow on the farm that makes noises like you, but it also gives milk.

You have a good voice—if you don't happen to like music.

When you sing people clap their hands—over their ears.

Of course your voice is pure. Every time you sing, you strain it.

Singers run in your family—and they should.

I've heard better sounds come from a leaking balloon.

Your voice reminds me of water being let out of a tub.

The best way to improve your face is to keep the lower half shut.

You throw yourself into everything you do? Please go out and dig a deep hole!

Your brain is so weak, you have to wear crutches under your ears.

Please make like a bee and buzz off!

Next time you pass my house—pass my house.

At least you're original. You make a new mistake every day.

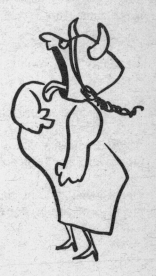

You're a natural musician. Your tongue is sharp and your feet are flat.

Your voice is as flat as your head.

I wish you were on TV so I could turn you off.

Your voice reminds me of a machine at home that sucks up dirt.

You couldn't carry a tune if it had a handle.

I love music—but please keep on singing anyway.

You say you sing with feeling. If you had any feeling, you wouldn't sing.

Your voice is heavenly—I mean, unearthly.

Do you know "The Road to Mandalay?" I don't mean sing it—I mean take it.

You sing like a bird and have a brain to match.

Anyone with a voice like yours ought to be arrested for disturbing the peace.

Signal when you're finished singing, so I can take my fingers our of my ears.

You do your singing in the shower? Don't sing very often, do you?

You could make a living hiring yourself out as a noisemaker at parties.

You could make a living souring milk.

You're the flower of manhood—a blooming idiot.

Dracula would turn you down. He wants plasma, not asthma.

Your mouth is so big, you can sing duets all by yourself.

After they made you, they broke the jelly mold.

The muscles in your arms are like potatoes—mashed potatoes.

You sing like a bird—a cuckoo.

You look pretty today—pretty awful.

You missed being Miss America by two feet: twelve inches on each hip.

You always seem to mind your business at the top of your lungs.

You have a fine voice. Don't spoil it by singing.

You sound much better with your mouth closed.

I'd like to rock you to sleep—with big ones.

If I ever want to remember your voice, I just tear a rag.

Your voice is too loud for indoor use.

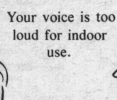

10 DOWN
with HIGH
NOON!

You're such a weakling, you couldn't lick a postage stamp.

You're so weak, when you let the bath water out, you can barely fight the current.

You look like you went to the blood bank and forgot to say when.

You're so popular, your picture hangs in 5,000 post offices around the country.

I haven't seen anything like you since the circus left town.

I hear you can trace your ancestors back to royalty—King Kong.

They said your baby brother looked like you. Then they turned him right side up.

There must be something about you that I like, but I can't stand close enough to you to find out.

You're such a blockhead, you should have termite insurance for your brain.

You keep opening things by mistake—mostly your mouth.

Are you always so stupid—or is this one of your better days?

I understand you. I have a way with dumb animals.

Why don't you play with your yo-yo and practice being a jerk?

Why don't you go to a cliff and jump to a conclusion?

Some people are hard-boiled. You're just half-baked.

All I can say is that you're in better company than I am.

That chip on your shoulder indicates a block of wood nearby.

Quick, put a helmet on your head! Here comes a woodpecker!

I wish I were a carpenter so I could fix your wagon.

Where did you get your brains—in a doll shop?

You ought to sue your brain for nonsupport.

You think you have an open mind, but that's only your mouth.

You have a concrete mind—permanently set.

The only thing you took up in school was space.

You are the only person I know who got a D in his ABC's.

The only polish you have is on your shoes.

I like the way you're dressed. Who wears your clean shirts?

When you went to school, the teacher played hookey.

I heard you just had an idea. Beginner's luck!

The nearest you'll ever come to a brainstorm is a light drizzle.

You only use your head to hold up your hat.

Don't be so smart. Remember, you can always be replaced by a human being.

Don't give me a piece of your mind—you can't spare it.

I hope you turn over a new leaf—and it's poison ivy.

When I look at you, time stands still. Your face would stop any clock.

I hear you were such a rotten kid, your parents ran away from home.

If I said anything to offend you, please let me know. I might want to do it again.

11 THE GREAT DEBATE

Is that your head, or did somebody find a way to grow hair on a meatball?

You may be thoughtless—but you're never speechless.

You may be outspoken, but I can't think of by whom.

Generally speaking—you're generally speaking.

You're someone who never goes without saying.

You're like a tugboat—the more you're in a fog, the louder you toot.

Better to keep your mouth shut and let people suspect that you're stupid, than to open it and remove all doubt.

The only thing you ever exercise is your tongue.

You have a tongue that would clip a hedge.

Your tongue is always sticking out, so why can't you hold it?

You use your tongue so much, you need a retread every six months.

Your tongue is so long—you can seal an envelope after you put it in the mailbox.

Your tongue is so long, when it hangs out, people think it's your tie.

I like the straightforward way you dodge the issues.

You never let the facts interfere with your opinions.

You have nothing to say, but that doesn't stop you from saying it.

You talk so much I get hoarse just listening to you.

You never learned to swim. You couldn't keep your mouth closed long enough.

Success hasn't gone to your head, only to your mouth.

Please turn off your mouth. It's still running.

You should try to get ahead. You could certainly use one.

Next to your head, the biggest bones in your body are your jaws.

Please close your mouth so I can see the rest of your face.

You have so much bridge work, anyone who kissed you would have to pay a toll.

You talk so much, even your tonsils get tired.

You ought to be on the Parole Board. You never let anyone finish a sentence.

You could make a fortune by hiring yourself out to fill hot air balloons.

Your main trouble is that you never make a long story short.

Your mind may be slow, but your mouth is fast.

I didn't say you had a big mouth, only that I saw you bobbing for basketballs.

You're the talk of the town—all by yourself.

We can always depend on you to start the bull rolling.

You're so full of bull, the cows must follow you home.

Chickens must like you because you're such a big cluck.

You couldn't tell which way the elevator was going if you had two guesses.

You're a person of few words—a few million words.

I liked you when we first met, but you talked me out of it.

Please close your mouth. It's getting hot in here.

If after a reasonable time your speech doesn't strike oil, you'd better stop boring.

You're the sleeping pill of the speaking profession.

You're not boring me. Just wake me up when you're finished talking.

You're such a bore. You won't change your mind—or the subject.

You're such a bore, even my leg falls asleep when you talk.

You always speak straight from the shoulder—too bad your words don't start from higher up.

Help prevent air pollution. Stop talking!

I've heard better conversations in alphabet soup.

Your ideas are so corny, they'd sound better with butter and salt.

If baloney were snow, you'd be a blizzard.

A brain isn't everything. In your case, it's nothing.

You have a point there—your head!

You're so narrow-minded, if you fell on a pin, it would blind you in both eyes.

You're so narrow-minded that if you put your brain on the edge of a razor, it would look like a pea rolling down a four-lane highway.

I have a minute to spare—tell me everything you know.

Some people can speak on any subject. You don't need a subject.

There are two sides to every question—and you always take both.

You're the decisive type. You'll always give a definite maybe.

Your speech reminds me of the horns of a steer—a point here and there, and a lot of bull in between.

 Just because you have a hole in your head doesn't mean you have an open mind.

12 MAN OVER~ BOARD!

If they ever put a price on your head—take it!

You're not really such a bad person—until people get to know you.

I've seen large windows, but you're the biggest pain of them all.

Just because you have a sunken chest doesn't make you a treasure.

If you stepped out to visit all your friends, you'd be back in a minute.

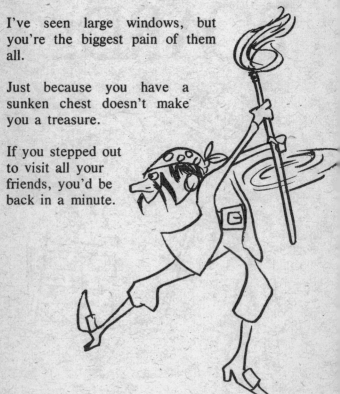

You have a heart of gold—yellow and hard.

Quick, get a hammer! There's a fly on your head.

You certainly have a nice personality. I think all your friends are wrong.

If you've got no place to go, I could suggest one.

What do you do for a living? You are living, aren't you?

You're perfect for hot weather. You leave me cold.

I'd like to see you in something flowing. Why don't you jump in the river?

Do you still love Mother Nature—in spite of what she did to you?

If you had your life to live over—would you please do it somewhere else?

You're so stingy, you won't even pay attention.

No wonder your brain is good as new. It's never been used.

If you're such a treasure, where did they dig you up?

You have ears like a shovel—always picking up dirt.

The only thing you should fear more than losing your mind is finding it.

You don't need to wear jewelry. You already have enough rings under your eyes.

I'd like to buy you two things for your neck: soap and rope.

If you won't have your hair cut, at least change the oil.

You're such a coward, you wouldn't even fight temptation.

You're such a coward, you'd be afraid to strike a pose.

You're a heel without a soul.

You were such a homely baby, your parents sent you back and kept the stork.

I'd like to give you something you need, but I do know how to wrap up a bathtub.

The only things that can stand getting close to y are fleas.

If I don't get in touch with you in a year or t' please show me the same consideration.

If I give you a scale, will you go weigh?

If I give you a rubber band, will you snap out of

Are you really leaving, or are you just trying brighten my day?

13 YOU WORM, YOU!

You know the old gag, "Your face would stop a clock?" Well, yours would stop a sundial.

I think of you often. But I'd rather not say what.

You must be sick. That can't be your natural appearance.

I was feeling fine until you came along.

I hear you won the King Kong look-alike contest.

When I watch you eat, I know where they got the idea for "Jaws."

What's wrong with you? How about if I gave it to you alphabetically?

You're like medicine—hard to swallow.

You look like a nervous wreck. Okay, so you're not nervous.

You're so weak, you couldn't even carry a tune.

You're so weak, you couldn't even bat an eyelash.

You're so weak, you couldn't even lick a lollipop.

If you tried to whip cream, the cream would win.

If you wore stilts, you'd still be a midget.

You're so short, when it rains you're the last one to know.

You're so short, you can pole vault with a toothpick.

You're so small, I couldn't even wipe my feet on you.

You're so small that when you take a bath, you have to wear snowshoes to keep from going down the drain.

Good things may come in small packages, but so does poison.

Didn't I see you once before under a microscope?

You're so short, you play handball against the curb.

You're so short, you can't tell if you have a headache or your corns hurt.

There's something about you I like. Give me a year or two, I'll remember it.

If I gave you a going-away present—would you?

14 SPEAK UP, DUMMY!

If there was an Olympics for stupidity, you'd break all records.

You were born with a big handicap: your mouth.

You remind me of decaffeinated coffee—no active ingredient in the bean.

You should wear a soft hat—to match your head.

You don't look well. When was the last time you saw your veterinarian?

I finally figured out what's eating you—termites.

I hear your family were the early Boones—the Baboons.

The only time you make sense is when you're not talking.

If a bird had your brain it would fly backwards.

The only thing your head is good for is to keep your ears apart.

Your ears are bookends for a vacuum.

If it weren't for your stupidity, you wouldn't have any personality at all.

Why don't you send your mind to the laundry?

 That's a nice outfit you're wearing. Didn't they have it in your size?

What's the matter? Didn't you like the food they gave you in the zoo?

You must have a clean mind—you change it so often.

You never change your mind? No wonder—no mind.

Know how to earn extra money? Rent out your head. It's empty anyhow!

Didn't I see you hanging around the faucet, you big drip?

Who wears your *good* clothes?

Now I know why you smile all the time. Your teeth are the only things about you that aren't wrinkled.

Does the undertaker know you're up?

I don't believe in talking to strangers—and you're the strangest person I ever saw.

Don't worry if your mind wanders. It's too weak to go very far.

In your case, an ounce of keep-your-mouth shut beats a pound of talking.

You say you have a mind of your own? Why don't you bring it around some time?

Do it tomorrow. You've made enough mistakes today.

You're so short, you have to wear socks to keep your neck warm.

You're so short, if you pulled your socks up, you'd be blindfolded.

You're not prejudiced. You hate everybody regardless of race, color or creed.

Use your head. It's the little things that count.

Why don't you deprive me of your company for a few years?

Your idea of a big evening is to take out the garbage.

You're so cheap, you even have your garbage gift wrapped.

The only thing you ever give away is secrets.

Of course I'm listening to you. Don't you see me yawning?

15 HAPPY VALENTINE'S DAY!

How much would it cost to buy back my introduction to you?

I don't know what makes you tick, but I hope it's a bomb.

You're neither right-handed nor left-handed—just under-handed.

The only prints you'll leave on the sands of time will be heel marks.

I wonder how you would look stuffed?

Would you mind reaching into your heart and getting me a piece of ice?

You remind me of a fine sculptor—a first-class chiseler.

You may think you're a bookworm, but you're only the ordinary kind.

You have such a turned-up nose, every time you sneeze you blow your hat off.

Tell me, if I gave you two aspirins, would you go away?

You may be a beautiful person on the inside. Too bad you were born on the outside.

You should have your face lifted—with a rope around your head.

You look shot—and that's what you should be.

There aren't too many people like you around. Thank goodness!

I'd like to say hello to you so that I can say goodbye to you.

Let's play Building and Loan. Get out of the building and leave me alone.

Let's play house. You be the door—and I'll slam you.

You remind me of an astronaut—always blasting off.

I'll forgive your rudeness—I know you're just being yourself.

You are definitely non-habit forming.

How many rocks did they have to turn up before you crawled out?

You're a real big gun—of small caliber and a big bore.

Your face reminds me of an unmade bed.

If you ever need a friend—buy a dog.

You must have been a surprise to your parents. They expected a boy or a girl.

You know, you could be arrested for trying to impersonate a human being.

Help keep the neighborhood beautiful. Move to a foreign country.

You have a split personality. Some days you're mean; other days you're plain miserable.

The only way you'll ever get polish is to drink it.

You were born ignorant and you've been losing ground ever since.

Your face could use a retread.

You must be a magician. You can turn anything into an argument.

There are going to be a lot of empty seats at your testimonial dinner.

You're the kind of person who lights up a room by leaving it.

You should go to a **phot**ographer and get your negative personality developed.

I'll say one thing for you: you have an even disposition—always mean.

When you ran away from home, your parents didn't find you. They didn't look.

You make a big impression on people; you step all over them.

Why don't you take a long walk on a short pier?

I don't know what's bothering you, but I hope it isn't catching.

You'd make a good contact person—you're all con and no tact.

Don't think—you could strain yourself.

I like your approach. Now, let's see your departure.

Let me say it has not been a pleasure meeting you.

You're a confirmed liar. Nothing you say is ever confirmed.

Keep your temper. I don't want it.

You really work hard at being difficult, don't you?

Put some variety in your life. Find something new to hate.

Your mind must be permanently closed for repairs.

Please don't ever change—stay as you are: rotten, stupid, cheap, evil, dirty, vicious, foul and diseased.

Why don't you crawl back into the woodwork with the rest of the termites?

Make like a snake and slither away!

16 TOOTH or CONSE~ QUENCES

You may become famous in history —medical history!

You're a real life saver. I can tell by the hole in your head.

They should cover you with chocolate, because you're nuts!

Whatever is eating you must be suffering from food poisoning.

When your grandfather was born, they passed out cigars. When your father was born, they passed out cigarettes. When you were born, they just passed out.

When you were born, your parents looked up your birth certificate to see if there were any loopholes in it.

You're a chip off the old block—a real blockhead.

What you lack in looks, you make up for in stupidity.

Keep talking. Maybe you'll find something to say one day.

They don't make money in small enough denominations to pay you what you're worth.

You're just what the doctor ordered—a pill!

Where did you find your mind—in the gutter?

Do you have a license to drive people crazy?

You're not hard of hearing, just hard of listening.

Your remarks may be pointless, but not your head.

Have you been to the zoo lately? I mean, as a visitor?

Stay with me—I want to be alone.

Is that dandruff on your shoulders or sawdust leaking out of your ears?

Why don't you make like dandruff and flake off?

Close your mouth before someone puts an apple in it.

Don't try to diet. There's no way to reduce a fat head.

You're in fantastic condition. In fact, I never saw anyone in your condition.

Did you fill in that blank yet? I mean the one between your ears.

Your clothes look pretty good considering the shape they're on.

You remind me of the Liberty Bell—half-cracked.

The last time I saw a face like yours, I threw it a fish.

You must be a great cook. You already have the pot for it.

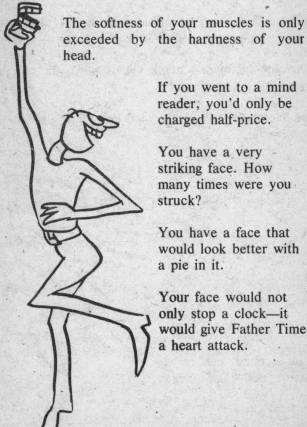

The softness of your muscles is only exceeded by the hardness of your head.

If you went to a mind reader, you'd only be charged half-price.

You have a very striking face. How many times were you struck?

You have a face that would look better with a pie in it.

Your face would not only stop a clock—it would give Father Time a heart attack.

You look like you had an argument with a freight train—and lost.

Why don't you get yourself a kitten? You could certainly use a new puss.

You're so narrow-minded, you can look through a keyhole with both eyes.

Even people who don't know you don't like you.

You may be high-strung, but not high enough to suit me.

Why don't you leave your brain to science? Maybe they can find a cure for it.

You could make a fortune helping people lose weight. One look at you and people lose their appetite.

Most of us live and learn; you just live.

When you die, *everyone* will rest in peace.

Remember, he who thinks by the inch and talks by the yard—deserves to be kicked by the foot.

Don't worry about anyone making a monkey out of you. Nature did it already.

I've got something in my eye that's painful—you.

Beauty isn't everything. In your case, it's nothing.

No wonder you've never been kissed—your mouth hàs never been still long enough.

You still have thirty-two teeth. Would you like to try for none?

Please make like a ball and roll away!

If you need me—hesitate to call.

17 oh, WHAT BIG EYES YOU HAVE!

Your eyes are like pools—sunken and watery.

Your lips remind me of petals—bicycle pedals.

You have calves that only a cow would like.

You may be as fit as a fiddle, but you look more like a saxophone to me.

If you went to the beauty parlor, they wouldn't let you in.

You must be older than you look. No one could get so dumb so fast.

I'm dumb? You spent two weeks in a revolving door looking for a doorknob.

You're not yourself today —thank goodness!

Stay with me. I want to be alone.

You're looks aren't half-bad. They're all bad.

You couldn't win a beauty contest if there were no other contestants.

You have an hourglass figure, but the sand has settled in the wrong place.

You have a schoolgirl figure, but it looks like it played hookey.

Your face reminds me of a flower—a cauliflower.

If you had a face, I wouldn't like it either.

You have a soft heart and a head to match.

Are you always so stupid or is today a special occasion?

Last night I dreamed I saw something in front of your house that made me very happy—a moving van.

Every time I pass a garbage pail, I think of you.

Please close your mouth, there's an awful draft in here.

What happened at your coming-out party, did they make you go back in?

You should be in the movies. You look better in the dark.

Do you go to school to learn to be so stupid, or does it come naturally?

You'd make a perfect model —for a dumbbell.

You dress well for someone who is obviously color-blind.

Is that your face, or are you breaking it in for Dr. Frankenstein?

You don't have enough sense to pull your head in when you shut the window.

The only thing that would whistle at you is a steam kettle.

You have a pretty little head. And for a head, it's pretty little.

That dress fits you like a glove. Too bad it doesn't fit you like a dress.

Why don't you go to a pet shop? Maybe someone will buy you.

18 WANT to EAT OUT?

What's on the plate, in case I have to describe it to my doctor?

Was the meal too spicy? Gosh, no. Smoke always comes out of my ears.

You're so fond of arguing, you wouldn't eat anything that agreed with you.

What's on your mind—if you'll forgive the exaggeration.

You're bright and early—well, at least, early.

The only quick thing about you is your watch.

The only thing you do fast is get tired.

Keep your words soft and sweet. You never know when you might have to eat them.

Of course I enjoyed the cooking. Do you have a stomach pump handy?

I'm now convinced it is possible to communicate with the dead. I can hear you distinctly.

You're not only wet behind the ears; you're all wet.

Why don't you stand up and give your brain a rest?

I know a perfect restaurant for you. They serve soup to nuts.

I'd like to tell you how I feel about you, but not while I'm eating.

You must be on a sea food diet. You eat all the food you can see.

It's not the ups and downs in life that bother me, but the jerks like you.

Better hide, I see the garbage collector coming.

You wouldn't say that if you were conscious.

The next time you wash your neck, wring it.

Are those your feet, or are you breaking them in for a duck?

You must be an actor. You're so good at making scenes.

Don't complain about the coffee. You may be old and weak yourself some day.

You're so lazy, you wait for the wind to blow your nose.

You're the perfect cure for anyone with an inferiority complex.

You're so tired at the end of the day, I bet you can hardly keep your mouth open.

Tell me, is your family happy—or do you still live at home?

You may be your own worst enemy—but not when I'm around.

I hear your friends threw you a big dinner. Too bad it missed.

Your kitchen is famous. It's the place where flies come to commit suicide.

Your face looks like you slept in it.

They put brighter heads than yours on matchsticks.

Even your TV-Dinners are re-runs.

There is nothing wrong with you that a brain transplant couldn't cure.

Your cooking would be fine if I were a termite.

You not only don't know how to cook, you don't know what's cooking.

You have a big mouth—and an appetite to match.

You must be a Minute Man—the way you stuff yourself. You've already had sixty seconds!

Listen to you eat. You sound like a soup-rano.

You eat like a bird—a vulture!

You really are cooking with gas. How about inhaling some?

You'd make a great football player. Even your breath is offensive.

Why don't you go on a diet and quit eating my heart out?

No one can stand you—but that's your only fault.

Does the Board of Health know you're running around loose?

I could break you in half, but who would want two of you?

It would take you five minutes to boil a three-minute egg.

You may aim to please, but you're a terrible shot.

There are two reasons why you don't mind your own business: (1) no mind; (2) no business.

A little bird whispered something in your ear. It must have been a cuckoo.

What are you *not* thinking about now?

As guests go, I wish you would.

If you must know, I'm ignoring you.

Where were you when brains were handed out?

Know how to lose ten ugly pounds? Cut your head off!

Don't go away mad—just go away!

19 YOU'RE STANDING on MY FOOT!

Were your parents disappointed? They must have wanted children.

The only time people treat you with respect is during "Be Kind To Dumb Animals Week."

The person who said all things must end never heard you talk.

You're so pale, the only way you get color in your face is to stick your tongue out.

You don't need much makeup. You have plenty of color from the diaper rash on your face.

Please breathe the other way. You're bleaching my hair.

Is that a new hairdo or did you just walk through a wind tunnel?

Tell me, did any children in your family live?

What would you say if I told you I had a bright idea?
   Nothing. I can't talk and laugh at the same time.

I hear they're making a study of your family tree. You must be the sap.

Please follow the example of your head and come to the point.

You pick your friends—to pieces.

Look, if you want to argue with me, I'll go out and check my brains, so we can start even.

You are smarter than you look, but then again, you'd have to be.

Some figures stop traffic. Yours only blocks it.

You had such a pretty chin, you decided to add two more.

Your ideas are like diamonds—very rare.

You have so many chins, you need a bookmark to find your collar.

You don't know the meaning of the word "fear"—besides the thousands of other words you don't know the meaning of.

No mind reader could read your mind. The print is too small.

When you go to the zoo, I hear the monkeys throw peanuts at you.

You have a memory like an elephant and a shape to match.

Don't feel bad if you have a cold in your head. At least that's something.

Having trouble making up what's left of your mind?

You have a schoolgirl complexion. It looks like it was expelled.

You have a figure like an hourglass. It takes an hour to figure it out.

You remind me of a banana without its skin—no appeal.

You have lips like cherries—and a nose to match.

That's some perfume you're wearing. Who sold it to you, a skunk?

The closest you'll ever come to being a classy dish is owning a set of china.

Oh, you're walking today! Did someone hide the broomstick?

You look like Monroe—not the actress, the President.

You had an idea once, but it died of loneliness.

Your clothes match your mouth. They're both loud.

You've known only one great love in your life—you.

Isn't it a shame you can't get anyone to love you the way you love yourself?

Dreamboat? You're more like a shipwreck.

The only big thing about you is your opinion of yourself.

You're so conceited, I hear you have your X-rays retouched.

Your idea of a real treat is to stand in front of the mirror and look at yourself.

Just what is it that you see in you?

You always walk with your nose in the air—that's to avoid smelling yourself.

Either your dress is too short, or you're in it too far.

You bought those clothes for a ridiculous figure—yours.

When you were poured into your clothes, you forgot to say "when."

You swim like a duck and have a shape to match.

The only thing that you can keep in your head is a cold.

You have hidden talents
—well hidden.

The only tense you use in speaking is pretense.

You're more than touchy—you're touched!

Tell me, when you go to the zoo, do the animals recognize you?

If ignorance is bliss, you must be the happiest person on earth.

Those words must come from your heart. They certainly don't come from your brain.

You're always sincere —whether you mean it or not.

If your I.Q. were any lower, you'd trip over it.

I don't know what I'd do without you, but I'd rather.

Lazy? Your idea of cleaning house is to sit in a corner and collect dust.

I'm sorry you didn't like my telling people you were stupid. I had no idea it was a secret.

Just because you are always harping on things doesn't make you an angel.

Just because you're always explod-ing doesn't make you a big shot.

Just because you have a pointed head doesn't make you sharp.

Look at you! Was anyone else hurt in the accident?

I understand that at Christmas they hang you up and kiss the mistletoe.

I think you're wonderful. But what is my opinion against millions of others?

INDEX